Brother Boniface

Baking with Brother Boniface

Wyrick & Company
Charleston

Published by Wyrick & Company
1-A Pinckney Street
Charleston, S.C. 29401

Grateful acknowledgment is made to Liturgy Training Publications for permission to reprint excerpts from *Clip Art For Year A (Year B; Year C)*; Steve Erspamer, Archdiocese of Chicago. Copyrights 1992, 1993, 1994.

Designed by Sally Heineman
Printed in the United States of America

Library of Congress Cataloging-in-Publication Data

Cover photos: Front, Michael Mauney; Back, Frank Bianco

This book is dedicated to

Rev. Msgr. Philip J. Franceschini

and the parishioners at

Our Lady of Pity Parish, Staten Island, New York,

who gave support for this book

out of their love for and friendship with

Brother Boniface and the Brothers of Mepkin Abbey.

Contents

Foreword

The first Trappist Cistercian Abbey in the United States—the Abbey of Gethsemani—was founded near Bardstown, Kentucky, in 1848. A century later, in 1949, twenty-nine monks from Gethsemani traveled to South Carolina to found the Monastery of the Immaculate Heart of Mary, later Our Lady of Mepkin Abbey, on the west branch of the Cooper River, about 40 miles from Charleston. The place itself had long been known as Mepkin, most likely a Native American word that meant "lovely" or "serene." The 3,000-acre tract was first recorded in 1681 in the name of Sir John Colleton, one of the original Lords Proprietors of the Carolinas. From colonial times until the early 1900s it was a rice plantation. In 1936, it was purchased by Henry R. Luce, the publisher and philanthropist, and his wife, the Honorable Clare Boothe Luce. Thirteen years later, the Luces donated Mepkin to the Trappist monks of Gethsemani.

In 1952, three years before Mepkin was raised to the status of Abbey, Brother Boniface Schnitzbauer joined the Order. Then in his mid-forties, he came to Mepkin from New York, where he had been a barber and co-owner of an ice cream parlor. He served the monastic community as its barber for several years. One day, one of the brothers showed him how to bake whole-wheat bread, and, as he tells the story, "Gradually I landed in the kitchen and there I got stuck between pots and pans for many years."

Brother Boniface doesn't like to talk about himself. Should you go fishing for a personal yarn by asking him a vaguely worded question like "How did you get from Germany to this country?" you'll hook the wry response "By boat." The sixth of nine children, he was born in Würzburg, Germany, on January 3, 1908. As he enters his tenth decade, he still speaks in heavily accented English. Since he was a U.S. citizen at the outbreak of the Second World War, he was drafted into the Army and sent to the Pacific, where he served for four years.

Brother Boniface does like to talk about baking. He remembers

ix

smelling the fresh yeast his mother used when she baked. He cautions bakers about their dough: "It shouldn't be too dry—or mushy either." He is pleased that all his breads freeze well (for two or three weeks), but he is quick to point out that they should be thawed slowly in the refrigerator and not at room temperature. While he agrees that bakers do have secrets, he is delighted to share recipes because he remembers how he collected them after he learned how to bake whole-wheat bread: "from relatives, friends, newspaper clippings, cookbooks—recipes that were changed many times from hand to hand."

When asked "What does it take to be a good baker?" Brother Boniface has a ready answer: "You've godt to have *gute* recipes."

This is a book of good recipes.

Preface

Monastic work, no matter what the assignment, is always a group effort. Someone gives the order, another or others perform the task, another cleans up, another follows to complete the task. This is the way a community works.

So it has been with this book. We came to the publishers with the idea. They offered advice. They gave to many testers, including some of the brothers, their tasks. When they finished their work, others came and tested their work. The production of this book has been a group effort.

We are especially grateful to Ms. Celia Cerasoli of Celia's Porta Via Restaurant in Charleston, who tested many of the recipes several times and offered helpful suggestions. Ms. Flavia Manske of Charleston volunteered her precious time from the Spoleto Festival Office to further the work. Mrs. Joseph Kline of Brigantine, New Jersey, and Mrs. Arthur Washburn of Pleasantville, New York, did a lot of baking, testing and tasting. Finally, our own Br. Edward Shivell did yeoman's work in the kitchen during the testing process. To all of these, we give our hearty thanks.

We hope that you enjoy this book and find it useful in your kitchen. It comes to you with joy and a sense of fulfillment from our own hands and hearts to yours. We have delighted in these recipes over many years. The foods described in this book, especially the breads, have helped form our community around the table of fellowship, mutual service and love. We have left our dining room happier and more committed to God and to our monastic brotherhood because of them. In sharing them with you, we pass on to you some of our own contentment and peace.

May God be with you.

Br. Boniface Schnitzbauer
and the Brothers of Mepkin Abbey

Yeast
Breads

Health Bread

Preheat oven to 375° (15 minutes before bake time).

Combine salt and honey in the bowl of an electric mixer. Add flour and begin to mix while adding 1 cup of warm water.

Dissolve yeast in the remaining 1 1/4 cups of warm water and add to the mixture.

Adjust with additional warm water to form a soft dough.

First Rise: Let rise to double its size, punch down and form into two round loaves.

Second Rise: Put in greased loaf pans (9"x 5"x 3") and let rise about 1 inch above the rim, or about 30 minutes.

Bake for 35 to 40 minutes.

Yield: Two Loaves. (Freezes well in plastic bags.)

4 1/2 to 5 cups (1 1/2 lbs.) stone-ground whole-wheat flour
1/4 oz. (1 tablespoon) salt
1/4 cup honey
3 pkgs. active dry yeast
2 1/4 cups warm water

French-Style Bread

6 cups of white high-gluten flour (bread flour)
2 teaspoons sugar
2 tablespoons salt
2 pkgs. active dry yeast
2 tablespoons butter or margarine, softened
2 1/2 to 3 cups of warm water (120°–130° F)

Cornmeal (to dust pans)

2 tablespoons sesame seeds
For egg wash: 1 egg white with 1 tablespoon water

Preheat oven to 375° (15 minutes before baking).

Mix 2 cups of flour with the sugar, salt and undissolved yeast. Add softened butter. Place in bowl of electric mixer. Gradually add warm water, and beat for 2 minutes at medium speed.

Stir in enough remaining flour to make a soft dough. Knead until smooth and elastic. Place dough in a lightly greased bowl. Cover with a cloth and let rise at room temperature until double (1 to 3 hours). Punch down, and let rise again to one-half size. Punch down and halve. Roll into 2 loaves and place about 3 to 4 inches apart on baking sheet that has been greased and dusted with cornmeal.

Let rest and rise again (about 20 minutes). Using a small sharp knife, cut small slits along the top. Brush with egg wash and sprinkle with sesame seeds. Repeat egg wash during baking.

Bake at 375° for 35–40 minutes, or until the loaves are golden brown and sound hollow when tapped. Remove to a wire rack to cool.

Yield: 2 loaves.

Pumpernickel Bread

Preheat oven to 375° (15 minutes before bake time).

Dissolve yeast in warm water and let sit a few minutes until the yeast starts to bubble. Add caramel coloring/water mixture.

Stir in rye meal, salt and caraway seeds.

Add enough bread flour to make a soft dough. Knead until smooth and elastic.

Let dough rise until double in size (approximately 45 minutes).

Divide the dough in half and use your hands to form two round loaves. Place on greased baking sheet that has been sprinkled with cornmeal.

Let the loaves rise again (approximately 30 minutes).

Prepare glaze by dissolving the cornstarch in 1/2 cup cold water. Add 1 cup of boiling water and mix. Brush the loaves with the cornstarch glaze before and during baking.

Bake 35-40 minutes at 375°, or until loaves sound hollow when gently tapped.

Yield: 2 loaves.

DOUGH
4 pkgs. (1 oz.) active dry yeast
2 cups warm water
1 tablespoon caramel coloring (dissolved in 1 cup warm water)
3 cups rye meal (unsifted rye flour) or pumpernickel flour
2 tablespoons salt
2 tablespoons caraway seeds
6 cups white high-gluten flour (bread flour)

Cornmeal to dust pan

GLAZE
1 to 2 teaspoons cornstarch
1/2 cup cold water
1 cup boiling water

Raisin Cinnamon Bread

4 pkgs. (1 oz.) active dry
  yeast
1 cup warm water
  (to dissolve yeast)
1/3 teaspoon salt
1 1/2 tablespoons cinnamon
1/4 cup butter or margarine,
  melted
1/2 cup honey
3 cups high-gluten white
  flour (bread flour)
1 1/2 cups raisins

Preheat oven to 375° (15 minutes before baking time).

Dissolve yeast in warm water, and let stand until bubbles begin to form. Add next 4 ingredients (salt, cinnamon, butter and honey) and enough of the flour to make a soft dough. Knead on a floured surface (to the count of 100) until smooth and elastic. With a wooden spoon add the raisins and knead to another count of 100.

Let rise and double in size. Punch down, and let rise another ten minutes. Form into loaf, and place in greased loaf pan (9" x 5"). Let rise about 1 inch above the pan. Bake on middle rack since cinnamon browns quickly.

Bake at 375° for 35–40 minutes, or until done. (If you tap gently on the loaf, it should sound hollow.)

Yield: 1 loaf.

Rye Bread

Preheat oven to 375° (15 minutes before bake time).

Dissolve yeast in warm water. Let rest a few minutes until mixture begins to bubble. Add sugar, salt, butter and caraway seeds. Stir in the rye flour. Add enough white flour to make a soft dough. Knead until smooth and elastic. Let rise and double in size. Divide into two, and roll into loaves.

Place in two greased standard size loaf pans (9" x 5") that have been lightly dusted with cornmeal. Let rise again until loaves rise 1 inch above the edge of the pan.

For glaze: Mix the cornstarch with 1 cup of cold water to avoid lumps, and then add the cup of boiling water. Mix well. Brush the loaves with the cornstarch glaze before and during baking.

Bake for 35 minutes, or until loaves are golden and sound hollow when gently tapped.

Yield: 2 loaves.

DOUGH
4 pkgs. (1 oz.) active dry yeast
2 cups warm water
1 tablespoon sugar
1 tablespoon salt
1 1/2 tablespoons butter or margarine, softened
1/4 cup caraway seeds (approximately 1 oz.)
1 1/2 cups light (not dark) rye flour
5–6 cups white high-gluten flour
Cornmeal to dust pans

GLAZE
1 tablespoon cornstarch
1 cup cold water
1 cup boiling water

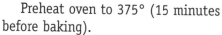

White Loaves

3 pkgs. (3⁄4 oz.) active dry
   yeast
3⁄4 cup warm water
3⁄4 cup warm milk
1⁄2 cup honey
3 tablespoons butter or
   margarine, melted
1 1⁄2 teaspoons salt
Approximately 5 to 6 cups
   white high-gluten flour
   (bread flour)

Preheat oven to 375° (15 minutes before baking).

Dissolve yeast in warm water. Add warm milk, honey, butter and salt. Add enough flour to make a soft dough, and knead on a floured board until smooth and elastic, or to a count of 200.

Let rise and double in size. Punch down and let rise again halfway. Roll into 2 loaves and place in 2 greased loaf pans (8 1/2 x 4 1/2-inches). Let rise to about 1 1/2 inches above the pan top.

Bake at 375° for approximately 35 minutes, or until the loaves sound hollow when tapped. Near the end of the baking time, lower the oven temperature to 350°. Remove from oven and let cool.

Can be frozen in plastic bags.
Yield: 2 loaves.

Whole-Wheat Loaves

Preheat oven to 375° (15 minutes before baking time).

Dissolve yeast in warm water. Combine warm milk, honey, molasses, butter and salt. Add yeast mixture.

In a separate bowl, combine the two types of flour and mix well. Add enough of the flour mixture to the yeast mixture to make a soft dough. Knead until smooth and elastic.

Cover the bowl with a cloth or plastic wrap and let the dough rise until double in size. Punch down, and let rise again halfway. Roll into 2 loaves, and place in greased standard size loaf pans (9" x 5"). Let rise to about 1 1/2 inches above the pan top.

Bake at 375° for approximately 40 minutes, or until the loaves sound hollow when tapped. Near the end of the baking time, lower the oven temperature to 350°. Remove from oven and let cool.

Can be frozen in plastic bags.

Yield: 2 loaves.

---

3 pkgs. (3/4 oz.) active dry yeast
1 cup warm water
1 cup warm milk
1/2 cup honey
1/4 cup molasses
3 tablespoons butter or margarine, melted
1 tablespoon salt
2 1/2 cups white high-gluten flour
5 cups stone-ground whole-wheat flour

Yeast Rolls

3 pkgs. active dry yeast
1/2 cup warm water
(to dissolve yeast)
3/4 cup hot (whole) milk
1/4 cup butter or margarine,
melted
1/4 cup sugar
1 1/4 teaspoons salt
1 egg
Approximately 4 cups high-
gluten flour
1/4 cup of melted butter
(for brushing on the top)

Preheat oven to 375° (15 minutes before baking time).

Dissolve yeast in warm water. Cool to lukewarm.

Mix hot milk, butter, sugar and salt in large mixing bowl. Stir in egg and dissolved yeast.

Add 2 cups of flour and beat until smooth. Gradually stir in more flour until dough leaves the sides of the bowl. Turn dough onto floured surface and knead until smooth and elastic (about 8 minutes).

Place in a greased bowl, cover and let rise in a warm place until almost double. Divide dough into desired number of rolls (12 or 24 rolls) and shape into small balls. Place on a shallow greased baking sheet, cover loosely and let rise until doubled (approximately 30 minutes).

Bake at 375° for 15–20 minutes, or until golden in color. Brush with melted butter or margarine after removing from oven.

Yield: 12 medium size rolls, or 24 small size rolls.

Crescent Rolls

Follow directions for Yeast Rolls. After the dough has risen to double its size, divide the dough into three portions and roll each portion into a 10-inch circle. Brush each circle with the melted butter.

Cut each circle into 6 wedges* and, beginning with the wide end, roll each wedge tightly and curl the ends to form a crescent shape.

Place the rolls on a greased baking sheet. Let rise until double in size and bake for 15 to 20 minutes in a 400° oven.

*You may sprinkle each wedge with grated cheese or a small amount of jam before creating the crescent shaped roll.

Yield: 18 crescent rolls.

Quick Breads

Apricot Bread

Preheat oven to 350°.

Combine flour, baking soda, sugar, salt and cinnamon in mixing bowl and blend well. Add remaining ingredients (oil, eggs and pureed apricots). Fold in chopped pecans and dry apricots.

Bake in a greased and lightly floured standard loaf pan (9" x 5" x 3") for about 1 hour, or until tester inserted in center comes out clean.

Yield: 1 loaf.

2 cups all-purpose flour
1 teaspoon baking soda
1 1/2 cups sugar
1/2 teaspoon salt
1/2 teaspoon cinnamon

1 jar junior size apricot
   baby food (approximately
   6 oz. or 3/4 cup)
1 cup vegetable oil
3 eggs
1 cup chopped pecans
1/2 cup chopped dry
   apricots (optional)

Banana Bread

1/3 cup unsalted butter or
margarine, softened
2 eggs, slightly beaten
2/3 cup sugar
1 3/4 cups sifted,
all-purpose flour
2 3/4 teaspoons baking
powder
1/2 teaspoon salt
1 cup mashed bananas
1/2 cup chopped pecans or
walnuts (optional)

Preheat oven to 350°.

Using an electric mixer, cream butter until smooth and glossy. Gradually add sugar, beating until light and fluffy after each addition.

Add eggs and beat, by hand, until thick and pale yellow in color (if using chopped nuts, add them now).

Sift remaining dry ingredients together and alternately add the dry ingredients and the banana pulp to the creamed mixture. Blend thoroughly after each addition.

Pour the batter into a greased and lightly floured 9"x 5"x 3" loaf pan.

Bake for 60 to 70 minutes, or until the tester comes out clean. Remove from oven and let partially cool in pan for an additional 30 minutes before turning onto a rack.

Yield: 1 loaf.

Cornbread

Preheat oven to 375°.

Mix all ingredients together and pour into a greased 13″ x 9″ baking pan or large iron skillet.

Bake at 375° for 20 to 30 minutes, or until top is golden brown.

Yield: 16 to 18 servings.

2 cups white bread flour
2 cups cornmeal
3 tablespoons baking powder
1 teaspoon salt
1/4 lb. (8 tablespoons) unsalted butter or margarine, melted
1 cup evaporated milk
2 cups whole milk
1/2 cup sugar
4 large eggs (to make 1 cup)

Date-Pecan Bread

3/4 cup chopped pecans
1 cup pitted, chopped dates
1 1/2 teaspoons baking soda
1/2 teaspoon salt
1/4 cup vegetable oil
3/4 cup boiling water
2 eggs
1/2 teaspoon vanilla extract
1 cup sugar
1 1/2 cups all-purpose flour, sifted

Preheat oven to 350°.

Combine nuts, dates, baking soda and salt in a mixing bowl. Add vegetable oil and boiling water. Let stand 15 minutes, then stir to blend.

Beat eggs slightly and add vanilla extract, sugar and sifted flour. Add to the date/pecan mixture and mix well.

Bake in a greased 9"x 5"x 3" loaf pan at 350° for approximately 1 hour.

Delicious served with cream cheese icing (see page 97).

Cool on wire rack.

Yield: 1 loaf.

Gingerbread

Preheat oven to 350°.

Sift dry ingredients together. Add milk to egg and beat.

Pour liquid into dry ingredients and stir until smooth. Add vegetable oil and molasses.

Pour batter into greased jelly roll pan (12" x 7" x 1" baking pan) and bake at 350° for approximately 30 minutes.

Cool on wire rack.

Yield: 1 loaf.

1 1/2 cups all-purpose flour
1/4 teaspoon baking soda
1 teaspoon baking powder
1/4 cup sugar
1/4 teaspoon salt
1 teaspoon ground ginger*
1 teaspoon cinnamon
1/4 teaspoon cloves
1/2 cup milk
1 egg
1/2 cup molasses
1/4 cup vegetable oil, such as Wesson®
*All the spices in this recipe are ground.

Holiday Bread

2 cups sugar
2 cups self-rising flour
1 teaspoon ground
    cinnamon*
1 teaspoon nutmeg
1 teaspoon cloves
3 eggs
1 cup vegetable oil
1 jar (8 oz.) baby food
    prunes
1/2 cup pitted prunes
    (optional)
1/2 cup black walnuts
1/2 cup English walnuts
All-purpose flour to mix
    with nuts
* All the spices in this
    recipe are ground.

Preheat oven to 350°.

Using a large spoon, mix sugar, flour, cinnamon, nutmeg and cloves. Add eggs, vegetable oil and pureed prunes. Add pitted prunes and nuts (which have been mixed with a little bit of flour to keep them from settling to the bottom). Pour into a greased and lightly floured 13"x 9" baking pan.

Bake at 350° (on the middle rack of the oven) for approximately 50 minutes.

Yield: 1 loaf.

Pumpkin Bread

Preheat oven to 350°.

Sift dry ingredients together. Make a well in the center and add vegetable oil, pumpkin and cold water. Mix well. Add eggs, one at a time, and blend. Fold in pecans.

Divide batter into two greased and lightly floured standard size loaf pans (9" x 5" x 3"), and bake for about one hour, or until tester inserted in the center comes out clean.

Cool on wire rack.

Yield: 2 loaves. (Recipe can be halved for 1 loaf and may be frozen for longer storage.)

4 cups all-purpose flour
3 cups sugar
2 teaspoons baking soda
1 1/2 teaspoons salt
1 teaspoon baking powder
1 teaspoon ground
   cinnamon*
1 teaspoon nutmeg
1/2 teaspoon allspice
1/2 teaspoon cloves
1/4 teaspoon ginger
1 cup vegetable oil
1 can (1 lb.) solid-pack
   pumpkin
2/3 cup cold water
4 eggs
1 cup chopped pecans
*All the spices in this recipe
   are ground.

Zucchini Bread

3 cups all-purpose flour
1/4 teaspoon baking powder
1 teaspoon baking soda
1 teaspoon salt
3 teaspoons ground
   cinnamon
1 cup chopped pecans
3/4 cup golden raisins
   (optional)

3 eggs
2 cups sugar
1 cup vegetable oil
2 cups zucchini, grated
2 teaspoons vanilla

Preheat oven to 350°.

Sift together the first five dry ingredients. Blend well. Add pecans and raisins. Beat together the eggs, sugar, vegetable oil, zucchini and vanilla until creamy. Mix thoroughly with dry ingredients.

Put in greased and lightly floured standard loaf pan (9" x 5" x 3") and bake for 1 hour, or until tester inserted in center comes out clean. Remove from oven and let cool in the pan for 10 minutes before removing.

Can be frozen in plastic bags.

Yield: 1 loaf.

Biscuits

Preheat oven to 400°.

Sift the flour, baking powder and salt together. Using your hands, work in the butter until the mixture is crumbly. Add the milk and mix.

Scoop dough up by large spoon sizes and drop onto a lightly greased baking pan.

Bake at 400° for 10 to 12 minutes.

Delicious with Old Fashioned Apple Butter (see page 91).

Yield: 10 to 12 biscuits.

2 cups all-purpose flour
1 tablespoon baking powder
1/2 teaspoon salt
1/3 cup unsalted butter or margarine
A little less than a cup of milk

Breakfast and Supper Breads

Braided Coffee Cake

Preheat oven to 350° (15 minutes before baking time).

Mix basic sweet dough and let rise for 30 minutes.

Cream butter and sugar until soft, creamy and light. Beat in eggs, one at a time. Add salt and lemon rind.

Combine the butter/sugar/egg batter with the sweet dough. Stir in citrons, raisins and nuts. Stir in enough bread flour to make a soft dough and let it rest for 30 minutes.

Divide the dough and roll into three long strips. Braid and shape the braid into a wreath.

Place on a greased baking sheet and let rise for 30 minutes. Brush with melted butter and bake at 350° for 30 to 40 minutes, or until golden brown.

Mix icing ingredients together until thick, smooth and creamy. Apply icing when the cake is cool.

Yield: 1 loaf.

BASIC SWEET DOUGH
2 pkgs. active dry yeast
    (1/2 oz.)
1/2 cup warm milk
1/2 cup white bread flour

BATTER
1 cup unsalted butter
    (1/2 lb.), softened
1/2 cup sugar
3 eggs
1 teaspoon salt
2 teaspoons grated
    lemon rind
3 1/2 cups bread flour
1/4 cup chopped citron
1/4 cup raisins
3/4 cup chopped pecans
Melted butter

ICING
1 cup confectioners' sugar
1 to 2 (or more)
    tablespoons boiling water
1/4 teaspoon vanilla extract
    or 1 teaspoon lemon
    juice

Brown Sugar Breakfast Cake

BATTER
2 cups all-purpose flour
1 teaspoon baking powder
1 teaspoon baking soda
1 teaspoon ground
    cinnamon
1/2 teaspoon salt
1 cup sugar
2/3 cup unsalted butter or
    margarine, softened
1/2 cup brown sugar
2 eggs, slightly beaten
1 cup buttermilk

TOPPING
1/2 cup brown sugar
1/2 cup chopped nuts
1 teaspoon cinnamon
1/4 teaspoon nutmeg

Preheat oven to 350°.
Mix all dry ingredients together and add butter, eggs and buttermilk. Blend thoroughly. Pour into a greased 9 x 13-inch Pyrex® baking dish.
Mix the topping ingredients and sprinkle over the batter.
Bake at 350° for 45 to 50 minutes.
Yield: 1 loaf.

Cherry Muffins

Preheat oven to 375°.

Beat egg until yolk and white are blended. Blend in milk and vegetable oil. Sift dry ingredients together and add liquids until the dry ingredients are barely moistened. (Do not over-mix; the batter should be slightly lumpy.) Add cherries and nuts.

Fill 12-cup greased muffin tin about 1/2 full for each cup.

Bake at 375° for 20 to 25 minutes.

Yield: 12 muffins.

1 egg, beaten
1 cup milk
1/3 cup vegetable oil or melted shortening
2 cups all-purpose flour
1 tablespoon baking powder
1 teaspoon salt
1/3 cup sugar
1 cup of pitted cherries (drained)
1/2 cup chopped nuts (optional)

Cranberry Breakfast Bread

1/2 cup (16 tablespoons)
   unsalted butter, softened
1 cup sugar
2 eggs
2 cups all-purpose flour
1 teaspoon baking powder
1 teaspoon baking soda
2 teaspoons salt
1 cup sour cream
1 teaspoon almond extract
1 8-oz. can cranberry sauce
1/2 cup chopped pecans
   or walnuts
Butter and flour for
   preparing baking pan

Preheat oven to 350°.

Using an electric mixer, cream butter and beat in sugar and eggs (add eggs one at a time). Add remaining ingredients (except cranberries).

Place one half of the batter in a greased and lightly floured 13 x 9-inch baking pan and spread the cranberries over the mixture. Top with the remaining batter.

Bake at 350° for 50 to 55 minutes. Cool at room temperature before serving.

Yield: 18 to 24 servings.

Dutch Babies

Preheat oven to 450°.

Break eggs into the bowl of an electric mixer. Blend at low speed, gradually adding flour and salt. Add milk and blend thoroughly.

Melt 3 tablespoons of butter in an 8 or 9-inch iron skillet in the hot oven. When the butter has melted, remove the skillet from the oven and pour the batter over the melted butter.

Bake for approximately 15 minutes until the crust is brown. (The sides and sometimes the center will puff up unevenly, which is the normal appearance.)

Cut the pancake into wedges and pour melted butter over to taste.

A few drops of lemon juice, lots of maple syrup and a sprinkling of confectioners' sugar are tasty additions.

Yield: 1 large pancake (2 to 4 servings).

3 eggs
1/2 cup sifted all-purpose flour
1/2 teaspoon salt
1/2 cup milk

3 tablespoons butter to prepare pan

Recommended toppings:
Melted butter, lemon juice, maple syrup or confectioners' sugar

Irish Soda Bread

2 cups all-purpose flour
2 tablespoons sugar
2 teaspoons baking powder
1 teaspoon baking soda
1/2 teaspoon salt
3 tablespoons unsalted
  butter or margarine,
  softened
1 cup buttermilk
1 tablespoon melted butter
1/2 to 1 cup chopped nuts,
  raisins and maraschino
  cherries

Preheat oven to 375°.

Sift together flour, sugar, baking powder, soda and salt. Cut in butter with a pastry knife. Add nuts, raisins and cherries. Add buttermilk and blend.

Turn onto a floured pastry board and knead for 1 minute.

Form into a ball and place in the center of a greased baking sheet. Flatten to about 1/2 inch by 6 inches wide. With a sharp knife, make 3 to 5 deep slits across the top.

Bake at 375° for 30 to 40 minutes.

Yield: 12 to 14 thick slices (great for dunking in coffee or tea).

Johnny Cakes

Mix all ingredients together until smooth.

Pour into a 9 x 13-inch glass baking dish and bake for 20 to 25 minutes, or until the crust is nicely brown.

Yield: 4 to 6 servings. (Great served warm with syrup or molasses.)

2 cups milk
2 cups all-purpose flour
2 cups cornmeal
1/2 cup melted unsalted butter
1/2 cup sugar
3 eggs
4 teaspoons baking powder
1 teaspoon salt

Mepkin Abbey Cinnamon Buns

DOUGH
2 pkgs (1/2 oz.) active dry
   yeast
1/2 cup warm water
2 teaspoons sugar
1 cup milk
1/4 cup sugar
1/4 cup butter, melted
2 eggs
5 cups bread flour
1 teaspoon salt

FILLING
1/4 lb. butter, melted
Cinnamon sugar (1/2 cup
   sugar mixed with 1 1/2
   teaspoons of ground
   cinnamon)
2 cups raisins, soaked and
   drained

Egg wash (1 egg beaten
   with 1 tablespoon water)

Preheat oven to 350° (fifteen minutes before baking).

Dissolve yeast in 1/2 cup warm water (105°-115°) with 2 teaspoons sugar and set aside for 10 minutes until mixture starts to bubble.

Gently heat milk, butter and 1/4 cup sugar in saucepan. Cool.

Whip eggs into milk mixture.

Measure flour and salt into a bowl. Make a well in the flour. Add milk mixture and yeast mixture into the well. Blend flour in with a fork until all ingredients are well mixed. The dough will be sticky.

Place dough on a work surface that has been lightly dusted with flour. Work dough with your hands until dough no longer sticks to your hands. See Note.* (Don't add more flour unless necessary.)

Place dough in greased bowl. Keep in a warm place and let rise until double.

After it has risen, place dough on work surface and roll into a rectangular shape 1/4 inch thick. Brush with melted butter and sprinkle with raisins and cinnamon sugar. (Reserve some cinnamon sugar if desired for topping.)

Roll lengthwise and cut roll into 14 one-inch slices. Place buns cut side down into 2 greased 9" round cake pans. Place buns close together (just touching).

Let rise in pan until double. Brush with egg wash. Bake at 350° for 30-35 minutes, or until golden brown.

After baking, while buns are still hot, sprinkle with remaining cinnamon sugar or drizzle with glaze.

Yield: 14 buns.

Note: This step can also be done with a paddle attachment on a mixer. Work until dough comes away from the side of the bowl and is no longer sticky.

GLAZE (optional)
1 cup confectioners' sugar
1 to 2 tablespoons (or
    more) boiling water
1 teaspoon lemon juice
Mix all ingredients together.
    If it is too thick to
    "drizzle," add a bit
    more water.

Pecan Loaves

DOUGH
2 pkgs. (1/2 oz.) active dry yeast
2 teaspoons sugar
1/2 cup warm milk
1/2 lb. butter (2 sticks), softened
2 tablespoons sugar
4 eggs, separated (reserve egg whites for filling)
4 cups all-purpose flour
1 teaspoon salt
Powdered sugar (for dusting)

FILLING
1 1/2 lbs. pecans
1/2 cup sugar
4 egg whites (reserved above)
2 teaspoons vanilla extract
3 tablespoons milk (if needed)

Egg wash (1 egg beaten with 1 tablespoon water)

Preheat oven to 350° (fifteen minutes before baking time).

Dissolve yeast in 1/2 cup warm milk with 2 teaspoons sugar and set aside for 10 minutes until mixture starts to bubble.

With an electric mixer, cream butter and sugar until soft and light. Add egg yolks one at a time and mix well.

Measure flour and salt into a mixing bowl. Make a well in the center and add yeast mixture and egg mixture. Work with a fork until all ingredients are well blended. Dough will be sticky.

Place dough on a work surface that has been lightly dusted with flour. Work dough with your hands until dough no longer sticks to your hands. See Note.* (Don't add more flour unless necessary.)

Divide dough into 8 equal portions (approximately 4 oz. each). Roll each into a ball and set aside.

Prepare filling:

Grind pecans in food processor. Beat egg whites until stiff, add vanilla. In a bowl, mix pecans, egg whites and sugar. Mix well. If needed, add milk to make a spreadable mixture.

One at a time, flatten each ball of dough and roll into a rectangle slightly smaller than 9" x 6". Dust with powdered sugar and continue to roll until 9" x 6".

Spread 1/8 of the filling on each loaf and roll loosely, lengthwise.

Place the 8 rolls, seam side down, on greased baking sheets. Let rise until double. Brush with egg wash.

Bake at 350° for 35 minutes, or until golden brown.

Yield: 8 small loaves.

Note: This step can also be done with a paddle attachment on a mixer. Work until dough comes away from the side of the bowl and is no longer sticky.

Cakes

Cinnamon-Apple Cake

Preheat oven to 350°.

Using an electric mixer, cream sugar, eggs and butter together until fluffy. Beat in flour, milk and cinnamon. Fold in nuts and diced apples. Pour into a greased and lightly floured tube pan.

Bake at 350° for 50 to 60 minutes.

Yield: 12 to 14 servings.

4 eggs
2 cups sugar
2 sticks (16 tablespoons) butter
2 cups self-rising flour
2 teaspoons milk
4 teaspoons cinnamon
1 cup chopped pecans
3 apples, peeled, cored and diced

Coconut Almond Cake

1 cup of solid shortening
such as Crisco®
(no substitutes)
2 cups sugar
6 eggs
2 cups cake flour
1 tablespoon almond extract
1 14-oz. pkg. grated
coconut
Flour and butter for
preparing cake pan

Preheat oven to 325°.

Using an electric mixer, cream shortening and sugar together for 5 minutes. Add the eggs and flour, alternately, until all is used.

Using a large spoon, stir in the coconut and the almond extract.

Pour the batter into a greased and lightly floured 9 x 5 x 3-inch loaf pan.

Bake at 325° on the middle rack of the oven for 60 to 70 minutes, or until tester comes out clean.

Yield: 16 to 18 servings.

Cranberry Cake

Preheat oven to 350°.

Using an electric mixer, cream sugar and eggs, adding eggs one at a time. Continue mixing with a spoon and add the flour, baking powder and soda, salt, sour cream, almond extract and nuts.

Pour one half of the batter into a greased and lightly floured 9 x 13-inch baking pan. Spread the cranberries over the mixture. Top with the remaining batter.

Bake for 50 to 55 minutes.

Cool before serving.

Yield: 1 rectangular cake.

1/2 cup unsalted butter, softened
1 cup sugar
2 eggs
2 cups all-purpose flour
1 teaspoon baking powder
1 teaspoon baking soda
2 teaspoons salt
1 cup sour cream
1 teaspoon almond extract
1 8-oz. can of cranberries, drained
1/2 cup chopped pecans or walnuts
Butter and flour to prepare baking pan

Friendship Cake

Named in honor of the friend who donates a cup of wine to get the fermented fruit started

FERMENTED FRUIT
1 cup Wine —Starter *
1/2 cup sugar
1 cup sliced peaches,
  with juice

BATTER
1 box Duncan Hines®
  yellow batter cake mix
1 pkg. (3 oz.) instant vanilla
  pudding mix
1/2 cup vegetable oil, such
  as Wesson®
4 eggs
3/4 cup chopped pecans
Butter and flour to prepare
  baking pan

The Starter is usually given by a friend. If not, use 1 cup of wine. After your first cake, you will have enough Starter for yourself and a friend. No special wine is needed, just the one that you use for cooking.

On the 1st Day:
Put the wine, sugar and sliced peaches in a one-gallon glass jar and let it sit in the refrigerator for 10 days, stirring once each day.

On the 10th Day:
1/2 cup sugar
1 cup crushed pineapple, with juice. Add the sugar and crushed pineapple with its juice. Let it stand another 10 days, stirring daily.

On the 20th Day:
10-oz. jar of maraschino cherries (drained and cut in half). Add the cherries and let stand another 10 days, stirring daily.

On the 30th Day:
Drain the fruit, saving all the juices. (The reserved juices become the Starter for a friend.)

Preheat oven to 350°.

Using an electric mixer on low speed, blend the cake mix and instant pudding with the vegetable oil, eggs (added one at a time) and drained fruit.

By hand, add pecans to the batter.

Pour the batter into a greased and lightly floured 9 x 13-inch glass baking dish.

Frost with Cream Cheese Icing (page 97).

Bake at 350° for 40 to 60 minutes.

Yield: 1 rectangular cake.

Freezes well.

Frosted Carrot Cake

BATTER
1 cup all-purpose flour
1 cup sugar
1 teaspoon baking soda
1/2 teaspoon baking powder
1 teaspoon ground
   cinnamon
1/4 teaspoon salt
3/4 cup vegetable oil,
   such as Wesson®
2 eggs, beaten
1 cup grated carrots
   (about 2 or 3 carrots)

FROSTING
4 oz. cream cheese,
   softened
1/2 lb. box confectioners'
   sugar
1/2 stick (4 tablespoons)
   butter or margarine,
   softened
1 teaspoon vanilla extract
1/2 cup flaked coconut
1/4 cup chopped pecans

Preheat oven to 350°.

Sift dry ingredients together. Add vegetable oil. Stir in eggs (one at a time) and add grated carrots. Mix well.

Pour in a greased and lightly floured 9 x 13-inch baking pan and bake for 45 to 50 minutes.

With an electric mixer, cream ingredients for frosting. Apply when cake has cooled.

Yield: 1 cake.

Name Day Cake

(Gesundheits Kuchen)

My Mutter made this for each one of us every year on our particular Name Day. May the good God bless her soul.

Preheat oven to 350°.

With an electric mixer, cream eggs, butter and sugar until fluffy and light. Add flour, baking powder and lemon rind.

Beat or whip it until the dough falls heavily from a spoon.

Bake in a 13 x 9-inch glass baking pan or fluted cake pan at 350° for 50 to 60 minutes.

Top with strawberries and cream for an extra delight.

Yield: 1 cake.

1 lb. (4 sticks) butter
1 lb. (2 cups) sugar
8 eggs
2 lb. (8 cups) all-purpose flour
1 oz. (2 tablespoons) baking powder
Grated rind of a large lemon
Butter and flour to prepare baking pan
Strawberries and cream for topping (optional)

Old-Time Molasses Cake

1/2 cup butter or margarine, softened
1/2 cup sugar
1 egg, beaten
3/4 cup molasses
2 cups all-purpose flour
1/2 teaspoon salt
1 teaspoon ground cinnamon
1 teaspoon baking soda
1 cup buttermilk

Preheat oven to 325°.

Using an electric mixer, cream butter and sugar together.

Blend in egg and molasses. Sift together dry ingredients and mix with creamed mixture. Blend in buttermilk.

Pour into a greased 13 x 9-inch baking pan or tube pan and bake for 40 to 50 minutes.

Can be served with whipped cream, lemon curd or apple sauce or sprinkled with powdered sugar.

Yield: 1 rectangular cake.

Pistachio Cake

Preheat oven to 325°.

Using a wooden spoon, stir and thoroughly mix the dry ingredients with the eggs, oil and sour cream.

Pour half the mixture into a greased 9 x 13-inch baking pan. Sprinkle half of the topping over the batter. Pour the remaining batter over the filling and sprinkle with remaining topping.

Bake at 325° for 50 to 60 minutes.

Yield: 1 rectangular cake.

BATTER
1 Duncan Hines® Butter
  Recipe Golden Cake Mix
1 cup vegetable oil
1 cup sour cream
1 pkg. (3 1/2 oz.)
  pistachio instant
  pudding mix
4 eggs

TOPPING
1 cup chopped pecans
1/2 teaspoon ground
  cinnamon
1 tablespoon sugar

Brunch Cake

BATTER
8 tablespoons (1 stick)
    butter
8 oz. cream cheese,
    softened
1 1/4 cups sugar
2 eggs
1 teaspoon vanilla extract
2 cups cake flour, sifted
1 teaspoon baking powder
1/2 teaspoon baking soda
1/4 teaspoon salt
1/4 cup milk

TOPPING
1/3 cup brown sugar
1/3 cup sifted cake flour
1/2 teaspoon cinnamon
2 tablespoons butter or
    margarine, softened

Preheat oven to 350°.

Using an electric mixer, prepare batter by creaming butter, cream cheese and sugar together. Add the eggs and vanilla extract.

In a separate bowl, mix the dry ingredients. Alternately add and mix the dry ingredients, creamed mixture and milk.

Mix topping ingredients together until crumbly.

Pour batter into a greased and floured 13 x 9-inch baking pan. Add topping and bake for 35 to 40 minutes on middle rack in 350° oven.

Yield: 1 rectangular cake.

Pound Cake

Do Not preheat the oven: Always start this cake in a cold oven.

Using an electric mixer, cream sugar and shortening. Add eggs one at a time, beating well after each addition. Add flour and milk alternately. Add vanilla extract.

Pour batter into fluted cake pan.

Bake at 300° for approximately 1 and 1/2 hours.

Yield: 18 to 20 servings.

Can frost with a Chocolate Icing (see page 97).

3 cups sugar
3 cups all-purpose flour
2 sticks (16 tablespoons) butter or margarine
1/2 cup (8 tablespoons) Crisco®
1 cup evaporated milk
6 eggs
1 tablespoon vanilla extract

Sunday Cake

1/2 cup water
1/4 cup butter
1 1/2 cups all-purpose flour
2 teaspoons baking powder
3 eggs
1 cup sugar
1 tablespoon grated lemon
   peel
Butter and 1/4 cup of fine
   dry bread crumbs for
   preparing pan

Preheat oven to 300°.

Bring water to a boil. Add butter and cool.

Sift together flour and baking powder.

With an electric mixer, cream eggs with sugar until fluffy and light. With a spoon, add dry ingredients, lemon peel and butter-water. Stir until blended.

Pour batter into a fluted or plain tube pan that has been buttered and sprinkled with bread crumbs.

Bake at 300° for approximately 1 hour, or until tester comes out clean. With a knife, loosen the cake around the edges and turn out onto a cake rack to cool.

Can be frosted with Lemon Icing (see page 96) or served plain with sweet whipped cream.

Yield: 16 to 18 servings.

Yum Yum Cake

Preheat oven to 350°.

Combine raisins, sugar, butter, cinnamon, nutmeg and water in a sauce pan and bring to a boil. Boil for 15 minutes.

Remove from stove and cool to room temperature. Sift dry ingredients together. Blend dry ingredients with the cooled liquid mixture and pour into a 9 x 13-inch greased baking pan.

Bake at 350° on the middle rack of the oven for 40 to 60 minutes, or until tester comes out clean.

Serve plain or with Custard Sauce (see page 93).

Yield: 18 to 24 servings.

1 pkg. (15 oz.) raisins
2 cups sugar
1/2 cup (8 tablespoons)
 butter or margarine
1 teaspoon ground
 cinnamon
1/2 teaspoon ground
 nutmeg
Grated lemon rind
 (1 medium lemon),
 optional
1/4 teaspoon grated ginger
3 cups water
3 teaspoons baking soda
3 cups all-purpose flour
Butter to prepare pan

Pies
and
Cream
Cakes

Cheesecake

Preheat oven to 350°.

Soften cream cheese at room temperature and add sugar gradually by alternating sugar with 2 eggs at a time. When blended, fold in sour cream.

Prepare crumb crust by mixing all ingredients and pack firmly into a 10-inch round spring form cake pan.

Spread cream cheese mixture over the crumb crust.

Bake at 350° on middle rack for 40 to 50 minutes. Turn off oven and continue baking for 1 hour.

Remove from oven and cool. Should be stored in refrigerator.

Recommended topping: Pineapple Sauce (see page 92).

Yield: 10 to 12 servings.

BATTER
1 1/2 lb. (4 8-oz. pkgs.)
cream cheese, softened
1 3/4 cups sugar
6 eggs
1 pint (16 oz.) sour cream

CRUMB CRUST
18 graham crackers,
crushed or rolled fine
1/4 cup melted butter
1/4 cup sugar

Cherry Pie

1 9-inch pie shell, baked

CUSTARD
8 oz. cream cheese,
    softened
1 15-oz. can sweetened
    condensed milk
1/3 cup lemon juice
1 teaspoon vanilla extract

GLAZE
2 tablespoons sugar
2 teaspoons cornstarch
1/2 cup cherry juice
1 cup drained red tart
    pitted cherries

Prepare oven and bake pie crust according to instructions.

Using an electric mixer, beat cream cheese until fluffy. Gradually add condensed milk and stir until mixed. Add lemon juice and vanilla extract. Stir until well mixed. Pour into the baked, and cooled, pie shell.

Refrigerate overnight. Do Not Freeze.

Prepare Cherry Glaze: Blend sugar and cornstarch in a saucepan. Stir in cherry juice and cook over medium heat, stirring constantly, until thickened and clear. Stir in pitted cherries. Let the mixture cool before pouring on pie custard.

Yield: 10 to 12 servings.

Crumb Pie Crust

Mix crumbs with butter and sugar. Evenly distribute the mixture in a buttered 9-inch pie plate by using the back of a large spoon to push the crumbs against the bottom and sides.

For recipes calling for a baked crust, bake the crust in a 325° oven for 10 minutes and cool before adding filling.

18 or more graham crackers, crushed or rolled to make 1 1/2 cups of fine crumbs

1/2 cup (2 sticks) melted butter

1/4 cup sugar

Custard Pie

**9-inch Crumb Pie crust
(see page 59),
uncooked**

**FILLING
3 cups milk, warmed
4 eggs, beaten
1 teaspoon salt
1 teaspoon vanilla extract
3/4 cup sugar**

Preheat oven to 425°.

Using a whisk or large spoon, beat eggs, sugar and salt together. Add warm milk and vanilla. Pour into the pie shell.

Bake at 425° for ten minutes to brown the pie crust. Reduce the heat to 325° and continue baking for 35 to 40 minutes.

Remove from oven and cool. Should be stored in refrigerator.

Recommended topping: Pineapple Sauce (see page 92).

Yield: 10 to 12 servings.

French Apple Pie

Preheat oven to 375°.

Prepare pie shell and set aside.

Peel, core and slice apples and sprinkle with lemon juice. Melt butter in a skillet and add sugar, spices and apple slices. Sauté for 5 minutes. Set aside until you complete the custard.

Combine brown sugar and tapioca in a saucepan over medium heat. Slowly add milk and bring to a boil, stirring constantly. Reduce heat and simmer until thickened (about one minute).

Add a small amount of the thickened custard to the beaten egg yolks. Add remaining custard and stir. Cook over medium heat until slightly thickened. Stir in butter and vanilla. Pour into a bowl and set aside to cool.

Pour cooled custard filling into pie shell and arrange apples on top.

Bake at 375° on the middle rack of the oven for approximately 45 minutes to 1 hour.

Yield: 8 to 10 servings.

1 9-inch pie shell, baked

CUSTARD
3/4 cup brown sugar
1 tablespoon tapioca
1 cup evaporated milk
2 egg yolks, beaten
1 tablespoon butter
1 teaspoon vanilla extract

APPLE MIXTURE
2 lbs. peeled, cored and
    thinly sliced apples
    (8 to 10 cups)
1 tablespoon lemon juice
2 tablespoons butter
2 tablespoons sugar
1 teaspoon ground
    cinnamon
1/4 teaspoon ground nutmeg

GLAZE
1/2 cup butter
1 tablespoon water
1 1/2 cups powdered sugar
1 teaspoon brandy
Vanilla extract to taste

Huguenot Torte

2 eggs, well beaten
1 cup sugar
1 cup baking apples,
    peeled, cored and finely
    chopped and firmly
    packed
1 teaspoon vanilla
Pinch of salt

Preheat oven to 350°.

Combine all ingredients and place in a greased 13" x 9" baking pan.

Bake at 350° for approximately 45 minutes.

Yield: 10 to 12 servings.

Napoleon Torte

Preheat oven to 350°.

Prepare pastry by mixing butter and flour with a pastry knife. Combine with egg yolks, sugar, salt and vanilla extract. Stir in milk.

When thoroughly mixed, form into 4 balls and chill in the refrigerator for 30 minutes.

Roll each ball on a floured board to 1/8-inch thickness and bake on greaseless flat cake tins (12-inch diameter) in a moderate (350° oven) for about 10 minutes, or until lightly browned. Prick dough before baking.

For Filling: Stir egg yolks in cold water and add to dry pie filling. Blend and add boiling water. Cook over medium heat until thickened. Stir in lemon juice and cool.

As it cools, stir occasionally to prevent a skin from forming on the top.

Using an electric mixer, cream butter while gradually adding confectioners' sugar, then cooled lemon custard. Beat well.

Spread the custard filling between the cake layers and on top and sides. Save one cake layer to be crushed into crumbs which can be sprinkled on the torte.

PASTRY
2 sticks (1/2 lb.) unsalted butter, softened
2 cups all-purpose flour
1 egg yolk
1 tablespoon sugar
1/2 teaspoon salt
1 teaspoon vanilla extract
1/4 cup milk

FILLING
2 egg yolks
1/2 cup cold water
1 pkg. lemon flavored pie filling
1 1/2 cups boiling water
Juice of a small lemon
2 sticks (1/2 lb.) unsalted butter
1 cup confectioners' sugar

Peach Cobbler

PASTRY
3 cups self-rising flour
2 1/2 cups sugar
2 large eggs
1 1/4 cups milk (or enough
    to make 1 1/2 cups total
    when added to eggs)

FILLING
1 lb. (approximately 2 cups)
    canned (drained) or
    fresh peaches (peeled
    and quartered)
Sugar (to taste) for
    sprinkling over fresh
    peaches

Preheat oven to 325°.

Sift and mix together flour and sugar. Combine eggs and milk (to make 3 cups of liquid) and add to the dry ingredients, stirring well.

Place the dough in a greased deep-dish pie pan (9 x 2-inch round).

Arrange the peach slices on the sweet dough and sprinkle with sugar if using fresh peaches.

Bake for 35 to 40 minutes, or until pastry is brown.

Pecan Pie

Preheat oven to 375°.

Beat eggs lightly. Add corn syrup, sugar, butter, vanilla and salt. Add pecan halves and mix carefully, trying not to break the pecan halves.

Pour into uncooked pie shell and place in oven. Turn heat down to 325° and cook for approximately 35 minutes.

Yield: 10 to 12 servings.

1 9-inch pie shell, uncooked

3 eggs, slightly beaten
1 cup light corn syrup
1 cup sugar
2 tablespoons unsalted
   butter or margarine,
   softened
1 teaspoon vanilla
1/8 teaspoon salt
1 cup pecan halves

Pineapple Pudding Pie

1 9-inch baked pie shell or
graham cracker crust
2 pkgs. (3 3/4 oz.)
instant vanilla pudding
mix
1 20-oz. can crushed
pineapple in syrup
2 cups (16 oz.) sour cream

For Crumb Pie Crust, see page 59.
Mix dry pudding mix with pineapple and sour cream.
Pour into baked pie shell and refrigerate for several hours until well chilled.
Serve with whipped cream topping.
Yield: 10 to 12 servings.

Pumpkin Pie

Preheat oven to 375°.

Beat egg whites and egg yolks separately and put aside.

Brush pie shell with egg whites (save leftover egg white for filling).

Combine all dry ingredients. Add pumpkin and egg yolks and any leftover egg whites. Add milk and mix well. Adjust seasoning to taste.

Pour into uncooked pie shell. Bake at 375° for approximately 40 minutes.

Yield: 10 to 12 slices.

1 9-inch pie shell, uncooked

2 eggs, separated
1 lb. can solid-packed,
    100% natural pumpkin
1/2 cup sugar
1/2 cup brown sugar
1/4 teaspoon salt
1 1/4 teaspoons ground
    cinnamon*
1 teaspoon ginger
3/4 teaspoon nutmeg
1/8 teaspoon cloves
1/2 cup evaporated milk
3/4 tablespoon cornstarch
* All spices are ground

Rhubarb Pie

1 9-inch pie shell, uncooked

2 cups diced rhubarb
1 1/2 cups sugar
2 tablespoons flour
2 eggs, slightly beaten
1/2 teaspoon salt
Butter to dot on top

Preheat oven to 400°.

Put diced rhubarb into a strainer and pour boiling water over it. Drain and put aside.

Combine rhubarb, sugar, flour, eggs and salt.

Pour into pie shell and dot with butter.

Bake at 400° for 20 minutes. Lower heat to 350° and cook an additional 10 to 15 minutes.

Yield: 10 to 12 servings.

Shoo-Fly Pie
Based on traditional Pennsylvania Dutch recipes

Preheat oven to 400°.

In a medium bowl, combine flour, cinnamon, nutmeg and cloves. Add sugar and salt. Cut in butter with pastry knife or blender until mixture resembles coarse meal.

Dissolve baking soda in boiling water. Add molasses and egg and blend.

Pour half of the liquid into the pastry shell.

Add 3/4 of the flour mixture and stir gently. Pour in the rest of the liquid and top evenly with remaining flour mixture.

Bake at 400° for 10 minutes. Reduce heat to 325° and bake until pie is set and crust is golden brown (about 25 minutes).

Yield: 10 to 12 servings.

1 9-inch pie shell, uncooked

3/4 cup unsifted flour
1/2 teaspoon ground cinnamon *
1/8 teaspoon nutmeg
1/8 teaspoon cloves
1/2 cup sugar
1/2 teaspoon salt
2 tablespoons butter
1 1/2 teaspoons baking soda
3/4 cup boiling water
1/2 cup light molasses
1 egg, well beaten
* *All spices are ground*

German Apple Torte

PASTRY
1 1/2 cups all-purpose flour
8 tablespoons (1 stick)
   butter or margarine
1/2 cup sugar
1 1/2 teaspoons baking
   powder
Yolk of 1 egg
1/2 teaspoon salt
1 teaspoon vanilla extract

FILLING
4 to 6 lbs. cooking apples,
   pared, cored and thinly
   sliced (12 to 14 apples)
Juice of one large lemon
1/4 cup ground cinnamon
   and sugar
Butter

TOPPING
1/2 cup sour cream
2 eggs, separated
1/2 cup sugar

Preheat oven to 350°.

Using a large spoon, mix the butter, sugar, baking powder, egg yolk, salt, vanilla and flour together. Add the flour last.

Spread the dough (which is the consistency of a cookie dough) on the bottom and sides of a greased baking pan. Push the dough with your fingers to spread it up the sides of the pan. Add a small amount of soft butter to help distribute the dough.

Arrange the sliced apples in an overlapping pattern on the pastry and sprinkle with lemon juice and cinnamon sugar. Dot with small pieces of butter.

Bake at 350° for approximately 25 to 30 minutes, or until the sides begin to brown. Have the topping ready to apply and return the cake to the oven to complete the cooking.

For Topping: With an electric mixer, beat the egg yolk and set aside. In a separate bowl, mix the egg whites until stiff, adding sugar in 1/2 teaspoon portions. Fold the egg yolks and sour cream into the egg whites.

Spread the topping over the apples and return to the oven until the topping begins to turn a light brown color.

Turn the oven off, open the oven door and let the cake stand a little longer. Cool to room temperature before serving.

Cookies
and
Sweet
Pastries

Almond Cookies

Preheat oven to 375°.

Cream butter and sugar together in electric mixer. Blend in egg and almond extract by hand. Add flour and almonds. Mix well and chill no longer than 1 hour. (Dough will get stiff if chilled longer.)

Roll dough 1/8th to 1/4th-inch thick and cut with a diamond-shaped or round cookie cutter.

Place cookies on a greased baking sheet and bake for 7 to 9 minutes.

Can be made into sandwich cookies with Vanilla Icing (see page 96) between or topped with a Sugar Glaze (see page 95).

Yield: 2 dozen cookies.

3/4 cup butter, softened
3/4 cup sugar
1 egg, slightly beaten
1 teaspoon almond extract
1 3/4 cups flour
1/2 cup almonds, finely chopped

Apple Crisp

**3 lbs. of cooking apples,
  peeled, cored and sliced
1 1/2 teaspoons ground
  cinnamon
2 tablespoons water
1/2 stick (4 tablespoons)
  butter or margarine
1/2 cup all-purpose flour
1/2 cup sugar**

Preheat oven to 350°.

Peel and slice apples. Sprinkle with powdered cinnamon and overlap the apples in a 9-inch round baking dish. Sprinkle water over the apples.

Using a pastry cutter or fork, mix the butter, flour and sugar together until crumbly. Spread over the apples.

Bake at 350° for 30 to 40 minutes.

Yield: 10 to 12 small wedges.

Basic Cookie Mix

Preheat oven to 350°.

Using an electric mixer, cream butter and sugar together. Whip in unbeaten eggs, one at a time.

Sift dry ingredients together and add to creamed mixture. Add milk.

Mix thoroughly and add your favorite sweetmeats, chopped nuts or candies.

Bake on a greased baking sheet for 12 to 15 minutes.

(See cookie glazes on page 95.)

1 cup (2 sticks) butter or margarine
1 1/4 cups sugar
3 eggs
3 1/2 cups flour
1/2 tablespoon cream of tartar
1 1/2 teaspoons baking soda
1/4 cup milk

Cheesy Apple Squares

1 1/2 cups all-purpose flour
1 cup brown sugar, firmly
   packed
3/4 cup butter, softened
1 1/2 cups graham cracker
   crumbs
1/2 teaspoon baking soda
8 to 12 thin slices cheddar
   cheese
2 1/2 cups cooking apples,
   peeled, cored and sliced
1/2 cup chopped pecans

Preheat the oven to 350°.

Mix the flour, brown sugar, graham cracker crumbs and baking soda until crumbly. (Set aside 1 1/2 cups.)

Pat remaining crumb mix into a greaseless 13 x 9-inch baking pan.

Place the cheese slices over the crumbs. Toss the sliced apples with the sugar and place on top of the cheese.

Sprinkle the remaining crumbs and nuts over the apples.

Bake for 35 to 40 minutes, or until golden brown.

Yield: 18 to 24 squares.

(Store in refrigerator.)

Chocolate Brownies

Preheat oven to 325°.

Melt chocolate and butter together in a small pot or double-boiler.

Mix dry ingredients (flour, baking powder, salt and sugar) together and add eggs, vanilla and nuts. Combine with the melted chocolate and butter.

Pour in a greased and floured jelly roll pan (12 x 7 x 1-inch baking pan) and bake at 325° for 25 to 30 minutes, or until the sides begin to pull away from the pan.

Remove from the oven and cool before slicing into squares.

Yield: 2 dozen squares.

6 squares or 6 oz. melted chocolate

1 cup unsalted butter or margarine

2 1/2 cups all-purpose flour

1 1/2 teaspoons baking powder

1 1/2 teaspoons salt

6 eggs

2 1/2 cups sugar

1 1/2 cups chopped pecans

Chocolate Squares

BATTER

1 cup butter or margarine

1 cup brown sugar

1 egg yolk

2 cups all-purpose flour

1 teaspoon vanilla extract

TOPPING

6 squares (6 oz.) semi-
sweet chocolate, melted

1/2 cup chopped nuts

Preheat oven to 350°.

Cream butter and sugar together in electric mixer. Blend in egg yolk and vanilla. Add flour and mix well.

Spread batter in a greased 15 1/2 x 10 1/2-inch jelly roll pan.

Bake for 20 to 30 minutes.

Remove from oven and spread immediately with melted chocolate and sprinkle with chopped nuts. Cool and cut into squares.

Yield: 2 dozen squares.

Coconut Macaroons

Preheat oven to 350°.

In an electric mixer, combine sugars, butter and eggs, and blend well. Using a wooden spoon, add coconut and vanilla extract.

Sift together all dry ingredients (except oats) and gradually add to the creamed mixture. Add rolled oats and blend.

Mold into small balls and place at least 2 inches apart on a greased cookie sheet.

Bake at 350° for 12 to 15 minutes. Yield: 3 to 4 dozen cookies.

1 1/4 cups light brown sugar
1 1/4 cups granulated sugar
1 1/4 cups butter or margarine, softened
3 medium sized eggs
1 1/4 cups shredded coconut
2 1/2 teaspoons vanilla extract
1 1/4 teaspoons salt
1 1/4 teaspoons baking soda
1 1/4 cups all-purpose flour, sifted
5 cups rolled oats (not instant oats)
2 cups chocolate chips (optional)

Cream Puffs

1 cup water
1 cup all-purpose flour
1/2 cup butter or margarine
Pinch of salt
4 eggs

Preheat oven to 400°.

In a sauce pan, boil water, add salt and butter. Stir in flour. Remove from heat and add eggs one at a time, mixing by hand. Be careful to beat each egg until well blended before adding the next one. Continue stirring until the dough is shiny and satiny and breaks away in strands. *The dough can be chilled for short periods of time before baking.*

Drop large tablespoons of dough (heaping the dough in the center) on a greased baking sheet, placing them at least 2 inches apart.

Bake at 400° for about 30 minutes, or until golden brown. Reduce the heat to 350° and bake 5 minutes longer. Test them by removing one: if it does not collapse, the baking is complete.

Remove and cool on a rack. When cool, cut off the top with a sharp knife or cut a gash in the side and fill with pudding, ice cream or custard.

Yield: 2 dozen medium sized puffs.

Italian Cookies

Preheat oven to 325°.

Put flour in large mixing bowl.

Add the sugar, margarine, vegetable oil, salt, eggs and all of the orange (juice, pulp and grated peel).

Sprinkle baking powder, nuts and raisins over the mixture.

By hand, mix all the ingredients together, gradually blending all into the flour until combined.

Rub a generous amount of oil on your hands and gently knead the dough.

Cover the dough and let stand for about 30 minutes.

Shape and twist a small amount of dough (one at a time) into a rope and twist into a knot.

Bake the cookies on a greased baking sheet at 325° until they are a light tan color. Do not let them turn brown.

Remove from oven.

While cooling, prepare Vanilla Glaze (page 95). Spread glaze on cookies and set aside to dry.

Yield: 2 to 3 dozen cookies.

1 1/2 pounds (4 1/2 cups) white flour
3 heaping teaspoons baking powder
6 whole eggs
1 orange
12 tablespoons sugar
1 1/2 sticks (12 tablespoons) butter
2 tablespoons vegetable oil
Pinch of salt
3/4 cup chopped walnuts
3/4 cup white or black raisins

Peaches and Cream Crisp

4 cups sliced peaches, drained
3/4 cup quick-cooking rolled oats
1/2 cup brown sugar
1/2 cup all-purpose flour
6 tablespoons butter, softened

Preheat oven to 350°.

Arrange drained peaches in 8 x 1 1/2-inch round pie pan.

Combine oats, brown sugar, flour and butter. Sprinkle over peaches.

Bake for 30 minutes.

Serve warm with ice cream.

Yield: 8 to 10 servings.

Pecan Fingers

Preheat oven to 325°.

Mix all ingredients (except pecans) with a pastry cutter. Add pecans with a wooden spoon to avoid crushing. Use hands to mold the dough into small finger shapes (about 1 teaspoon of dough per "finger").

Bake on a greaseless baking sheet until golden brown, 12 to 15 minutes.

While warm, roll in confectioners' sugar that is sprinkled on waxed paper (or toss in a plastic bag to coat and store).

Yield: 3 dozen cookies (will freeze well up to 1 month).

DOUGH
1 stick (8 tablespoons) unsalted butter
1 teaspoon vanilla extract
2 tablespoons sugar
1 cup sifted flour
1 cup pecans, finely chopped

COATING
1/2 cup confectioners' sugar

Sand Tortes

BATTER
6 eggs
Grated lemon rind
1 cup all-purpose flour
4 tablespoons cornstarch
1/2 cup butter, melted

TOPPING
Chopped or slivered
    almonds (or chopped
    pecans)
1/2 cup sugar

Preheat oven to 350°.

Cream eggs and sugar in electric mixer until light and fluffy.

Add grated lemon rind, flour, cornstarch and a little less than 1/2 cup of melted butter, and mix by hand.

Place the batter in a greased spring form pan dish and sprinkle with nuts and then sugar.

Bake at 350° for 30 to 35 minutes, or until golden brown.

Yield: 10-12 servings.

Shortbread Fingers

Preheat oven to 350°.

Cream butter and vanilla together until soft. Add eggs and blend.

Sift flour, salt and sugar together and add to the cream mixture. Blend well. Add crushed noodles. Mix and chill for 2 hours.

Pinch off dough and roll on floured board to shape the length of an index finger. Brush the "fingers" with melted butter.

Bake at 350° for 10 to 15 minutes, or until golden brown.

Sprinkle with powdered sugar for an extra treat.

Yield: 5 to 6 dozen.

2 cups chow mein noodles, crushed to make 1 cup
2 cups unsalted butter, softened
2 eggs
1 cup sugar
2 teaspoons vanilla
1/2 teaspoon salt
4 cups all-purpose flour, sifted
1/2 cup melted butter for brushing the top

Sauces,
Glazes
and
Icings

Old-Fashioned Apple Butter

Preheat oven to 350°.
Mix all ingredients together and pour in a 9 x 13-inch baking pan. Bake for 1/2 hour, or until the mixture becomes thick and clear.

7 cups smooth apple sauce
5 cups brown sugar
1 teaspoon cinnamon
1/2 teaspoon ground cloves
1 cup apple cider vinegar

Orange Sauce

Blend sugar, salt, cornstarch, orange rind and cinnamon in a saucepan.

Slowly add orange juice and lemon juice.

Heat to boiling temperature and cook about 5 minutes, or until thickened, stirring constantly.

Yield: 1 cup of sauce.

Can be used hot or cold.

3 tablespoons sugar
Dash of salt
1 tablespoon cornstarch
Dash of ground cinnamon
1 teaspoon grated orange rind
1 cup orange juice
1 teaspoon lemon juice

Pineapple Sauce

2 tablespoons cornstarch
Dash of salt
1/2 teaspoon ground ginger
2 teaspoons lemon juice
1 20-oz. can pineapple tidbits
1/2 cup slivered maraschino
  cherries

Stir cornstarch, salt and ginger into a sauce pan. Add pineapple tidbits, lemon juice and cherries. Cook over moderate heat, stirring constantly until smooth and thickened.

Chocolate Sauce

Mix sugar, cocoa and cornstarch with cold water. Stir until smooth. Add boiling water and stir constantly to blend. Cook over medium heat until thickened. Remove from heat and add butter, vanilla extract and salt.

1 cup cold water
1 cup sugar
7 tablespoons cocoa
1 1/2 tablespoons corn-
  starch
1 pint (2 cups) boiling water
Salt to taste
1/2 teaspoon vanilla extract
6 tablespoons butter

Custard Sauce

Prepare vanilla pudding with milk according to package directions. Remove from heat, cool and add vanilla extract.

1 pkg. (4 3/4 oz.) vanilla
  pudding and pie mix
3 3/4 cups milk
1 1/2 teaspoons vanilla
  extract

Sauces for Cakes

1 cup cold water
1 cup sugar
7 tablespoons cocoa
1 1/2 tablespoons
   cornstarch
1 pint (2 cups) boiling
   water
Salt to taste
1/2 teaspoon vanilla extract
6 tablespoons butter

• Caramel Sauce

Mix sugar, cocoa and cornstarch with cold water. Stir until smooth. Add boiling water and stir constantly to blend. Cook over medium heat until thickened. Remove from heat and add butter, vanilla extract and salt.

3/4 cup of sugar
2 tablespoons cornstarch
3 cups boiling water
Salt to taste
4 tablespoons butter
3/4 teaspoon vanilla extract

• Vanilla Sauce

In a medium sauce pan, combine the sugar and cornstarch. Add boiling water and cook over medium high heat, stirring constantly until the mixture is clear and there is no starchy flavor, or about 25 minutes. Remove from heat and add vanilla extract, salt and butter. Cool.

Glazes for Cookies

• Vanilla Glaze
Combine 1 cup of confectioners' sugar, 1 tablespoon milk and 1 teaspoon of vanilla extract. Beat until smooth.

• Sugar Glaze
Combine and stir until smooth 1 lb. box of confectioners' sugar, 1 teaspoon vanilla extract and 4 tablespoons of softened butter or margarine.
Heat 1/2 cup of milk until warm and gradually add the sugar mixture until thin enough to spread.

Cake Icings

- Vanilla or Plain Icing

  Combine 1 1/2 boxes of confectioners' sugar, 4 teaspoons of milk (or more if it is too thick), 1/2 teaspoon of vanilla extract and 4 tablespoons of softened butter. Blend until smooth.

- Lemon Icing

  Using an electric mixer or beater, combine 2 cups of confectioners' sugar, 1/4 cup of soft butter or margarine, 1 teaspoon of lemon extract and a few drops of hot water until smooth and fluffy.

- 4-Minute Icing

  In a small sauce pan, combine 1 cup sugar, 1 tablespoon cocoa, 1/3 cup of milk, 1 tablespoon of white corn syrup (such as Karo®), 4 tablespoons of softened butter or margarine and a pinch of salt. Cook over medium heat, stirring constantly, for 3 to 4 minutes. Remove from heat. Cool and add 1 teaspoon of vanilla extract.

- Cream Cheese Icing

With an electric beater, combine and mix 8 oz. of softened cream cheese, 1 box of confectioners' sugar, 8 tablespoons of softened butter or margarine and 2 teaspoons of vanilla extract. Carefully fold in 1 cup of coconut and 1/2 cup of chopped pecans.

- Chocolate Icing

In a double boiler, combine 2 tablespoons water, 1 tablespoon butter, 2 tablespoons cocoa and 1 tablespoon of light corn syrup. Heat slowly (do not boil) and stir constantly until all ingredients are completely dissolved. Remove from heat and add powdered sugar. Stir until the mixture is smooth.

Always apply icing while the cake is warm.

Index

Pineapple Pudding Pie, 66
Pineapple Sauce, 92
Pistachio Cake, 49
Pound Cake, 51
Pumpernickel Bread, 5
Pumpkin Bread, 21
Pumpkin Pie, 67
Raisin Cinnamon Bread, 6
Rhubarb Pie, 68
Rye Bread, 7
Sand Tortes, 86
Shoo-Fly-Pie, 69
Shortbread Fingers, 87
Sunday Cake, 52
Vanilla Sauce, 94
White Loaves, 8
Whole-Wheat Loaves, 9
Yeast Rolls, 10
Yum Yum Cake, 53
Zucchini Bread, 22